THE BOOK OF HOURS

POEMS FOR THE EARTHQUAKE SURVIVORS FEBRUARY 2023 IN TÜRKIYE AND SYRIA

BY RTB

© Sunwyse Writing and Celebrancy Services 2023

Except for brief quotations in critical articles and reviews, this book may not be reproduced in whole or in part by any means without the prior written permission of the publisher.

ISBN: 978-0-6457648-0-2

Cover Images: Shutterstock

Design & Artwork:
Purple Possum Design
purplepossumdesign.com.au

'Found poems' are constructed from words already written which are then gathered together by the poet and reframed. I found these poems in the words of survivors, rescuers, and reporters as narrated by television and social media. As I searched for their details, I found more and more. I could not tell them all, and in those I have told, I have used my imagination to excavate the experiences and imagine what it might feel like for those who survived and were rescued, and those rescuing them. I hope the untold stories have also found their way into these constructions, and so have used first names to allow for other identities to find their way in. I hope these survivors will know that I have undertaken this writing with great respect and that it will go some way into garnering ongoing support for the victims of the earthquakes in Syria and Turkey. All profits from this collection will be donated to the UNHCR to assist the more than 300 000 people who have been displaced in this disaster.

THE BOOK OF HOURS[1]

According to the professor of disasters and health
at University College London,
while there is a precedent for people surviving
for many days after earthquakes, it is unusual.
What is usual? Our bodies are resilient
but there is a "hierarchy of needs".
Three minutes without oxygen.
Three days (72 hours) without water.
Three weeks (504 hours) without food.
Without these things we cannot survive.
In science, there are no miracles.

THE COUNTING BEGINS[2]

They say we are heroes,
Devlet and I, who am called Gazwal,
because we did not leave
but we are neonatal nurses
in the hospital of Gaziantrep
and this is what we do,
we look after neonates,
babies born too early
and if they could not run out themselves,
how could we run out on them?

I have never felt such tremours,
that a building of bricks and mortar and glass and steel
could convulse in an epileptic seizure
like a thing alive. So we wrapped our arms
around the cribs and held on as hard as we could.

I see the footage played back,
I see how little we could do,
two nurses to hold two cots –
there are a dozen cots in that ward
and we did not have enough arms
to hold them all.
We could not stop them shaking,
we could not stop shaking,
we are shaking still.

TWO HOURS[3]

My name is Taha, I am 17 years old
and this is the last video I will make.
I hope my family are alive to see it
because there are many things
I want to tell them before I die.
It was the shaking of the world that woke me,
the shaking of Adiyaman and I do not know
if our town still stands. Perhaps it was only
our home, perhaps it was only my room.
I hope that my family lives
and this message will find them.
It is the last video I will make.
The shaking begins again
so I will say these things more quickly
before I die. And while I still have room.
These are aftershocks, I think, that press
the room in closer yet, squeezing me among
concrete and twisted steel.

Death comes when we least expect it,
there are many things I regret.
What is there to regret but not loving well enough,
not helping my family whenever I could,
not being the big brother my sister deserved,
watching my phone instead of watching the baby,
not changing the world as I had hoped to?
These things I regret.
I regret when I have hurt others.
These are the things we will all regret
when death comes when we least expect it
and there is no time to make things right.
When there is no time left for regret.

So I will tell you that I love you.
I will tell you that my family is all that matters.
I will tell you that I wish for you all good things.
I will tell Allah that, God willing, if I should survive
I will live my best life. Whatever is asked of me.

FOUR HOURS [4]

There are hands that find their way
through the rubble like rats searching
for food, and I call to them,
they call back, we call back and forth
like birds singing in the forest,
our songs echoing, bouncing off crushed walls,
a raucous dawn cacophony
that wakes the dead.

Hands reach beneath my shoulders,
and I cry at the pain, I cry at the joy,
I cry at the pain as they drag me out,
not knowing my legs are stuck beneath,
they keep pulling and I keep coming
and there is less skin but the blood
flows back into my feet and I feel them again
and I cry for the pain and I cry for the joy
as they cradle me upward,
passed arms to arms all shouting all laughing
and there, there is one I know,
my aunt is among them
and she will take me home.

10 HOURS [5]

Boom-boom-boom
the building went down
floor by floor
on top of us

I, Zeligha, kept yelling for Taha
I wanted us all to die together
One family always together
My husband Ali
My children
Taha Semanur Yigit

Semanur and Yigit, they were asleep
in the room with us
but Taha, I could not reach
He could not hear me
I could not hear him
We thought he is dead
He thought we are dead

We went to my sister's home
Taha was there
Taha had survived
The world was mine at that moment
I have nothing but my family
I have everything

Our neighbours dug us out
with bare hands and picks,
with sledge-hammers and shovels,
kept digging and digging and digging,
not knowing if they would find living souls
or corpses of those they had nodded to in the street
every day as we passed each other by.

Now we are living in a tent
with hundreds of thousands of others
who have survived but have no home,
but we have our family
so we have everything.
Others have lost more.

We watch as they dig up
our home with machinery, not hands,
our homes demolished and dumped
into trucks to cart them away.
We watch the life we shared
dug up and carted away.
Together, we walk back
to the refugee tent
that is now our home.

ALSO 10 HOURS [6]

When the earthquake happened,
we were okay. I had to see if the rest
of my family were okay. I rushed around
to the home of my aunt and uncle
and saw it had collapsed. Five storeys
that had looked so strong, like
broken eggs upon the ground.

We dug through the rubble for hours,
the rescuers and other cousins who had come,
looking and hoping and looking,
while the rain lashed down on us
like angry tears.

I was tired. I had to rest. I sat down nearby.
The rescuers called me over then,
they had found a body.
It was my cousin Afraa, she was dead.
She had been due to give birth
She and my wife both due to give birth
and we had planned for our children
to grow up together loving each other
as our family knew how to do.
My heart felt as crushed as the building.

We heard a baby crying.
How can that be such a beautiful sound.
We scrabbled at the sand and the rubble,
digging with our bare hands,
removing the sand that covered the baby,
hid this newborn from our view.

The baby was still tied to Afraa.
I took a blade from my pocket,
cut the umbilical chord,
gave the baby to another cousin
and we rushed her to a nearby hospital
who told us that the baby was in good health
but they had no room for her.

We drove to another hospital in nearby Afrin
but it had no more room. We drove to another
hospital that was full. We kept driving
to the children's hospital where they kept her safe.

We had thought she was a boy first,
and told the doctors to name him Abdullah
after my uncle who had died in the quake,
but we are allowed to adopt her now
and she will be called Afraa for her mother
who gave her life at the same time as she lost hers.
The nurses at the hospital, they called her Aya,
which means a sign from God.
She will probably always be known as Aya.
Her name matters less than that she lives.
My name is Khalil. Do names matter?

Two days after Afraa died and Afraa was born,
my wife delivered our daughter, Attaa,
and she feeds them like twins.
So many others wanted to adopt Afraa
because she was a sign from God,
they came to the hospital claiming
they were related to her. I think they may
have lost children in the earthquake
or perhaps they sought fame,
because Afraa was known to the world,
but they did not know the right names
to take her.
I went every day
because I was afraid
that someone would steal her away,
our sign from God.

Now she will live with us, with my wife and I,
and our four daughters
and I will not make any difference
between her and my children.
She will be dearer because she keeps the memory
of my brother, of his wife, of my aunt and uncle.

I ask my children
should we give away Afraa
to those who want to adopt her
and in one voice they tell me no.
She is ours. Our sign from God.

14 HOURS[7]

They found me first, I am Nilay,
I was trapped beneath seven stories.
Strangers' hands pulled me out,
poured water into my mouth,
put bandages on me, stuck needles in me,
I knew I lived but I felt dead
because my family was still missing.

Next, they found Nil, she is only four years old,
when she sobbed into my shoulder
that bought me back to life, a part of life.

When they dug out my husband, Cengiz,
another part of my heart began to beat again
and we waited, that Allah might give back
our other children. We waited.

Alin, Alin! Your name will be ever on my lips,
calling you to me, they found your body
but not your spirit. Two years you had with us,
and now you are gone, but I will always call to you
and sing your name. We could not find
your sister's body, but we knew
our baby Birce was with you in death.

90 HOURS [8]

My name is Ibrahim
I am 23 years old
I was at home in Jableh in Syria,
in two rooms on the first floor,
with my mother, who is called Duha,
and my sister, who was to be married
in three months time.

When the floor beneath began shaking,
my mother and my sister embraced each other
and then everything collapsed, walls crumbling like cake,
dust returning to dust.

I called to my sister and my mother,
they were buried nearby, we could not see each other
but we could hear each other.
My sister was in a lot of pain.
She said she could not bear it anymore.
She did not know what to do. I did not know what to do.
After half an hour, she was silenced.
She was dead.

I did not know if I was alive or dead.
It did not feel real.
I thought I must be dreaming.
I could not tell day from light.
I think my mind was shutting down,
lights out inside my head
as well as outside.

When I could think,
I would lick the water dripping
down the wall I leant against
and then I would be lost again
somewhere in-between
life and death.

Now I have been reborn.
A new life. A new start.
There is nothing old left,
it must all be made new.

My mother does not understand.

MORE THAN 90 HOURS [9]

My baby's name is Yagiz, it means brave one,
when we named him, we did not know
how brave he must be.
He was only six days old
when the earthquake buried us.
I was breast-feeding him at 4:17am
(mothers look at the clock to see what time they are feeding)
when our home began to shake.
My husband was holding our 3 year old son
and we walked towards each other,
me, Necla, with Yagiz in my arms,
Irfan with Yigit, but the earthquake
got bigger and bigger
and the building was shifting
and the wardrobe struck us
and I fell with Yagiz clutched to me
and when we stopped falling,
I called out to my husband and child
but there was no answer.
I thought they were dead.

It was black night, blacker
than I had known night could be
when there are no stars and no
light from a clock or a computer or a phone
just black black black
The wardrobe was beside us, I could feel it,
and that stopped the concrete
from crushing us.

Yagiz was crying,
he had not finished feeding.
I held him to my breast
and he fed
and he slept,
A baby's world is simpler than ours,
he fed, he slept, perhaps
sometimes, I slept as well.
There was no sound, no light, just the feel
of my baby clutched against me,
the sound of his breathing, and mine,
sometimes he cried.
We could not move in the space we were in
but he felt safe in my arms.

When I heard voices
I thought I dreamed it
but I kept hearing them
and I began screaming for help.
Is anyone there? Can anyone hear me?
I shouted. I screamed. I shouted.
I banged on the wardrobe with bits of rock,
it was splintering the wardrobe
that had protected us. I kept banging.
Is there anyone there? Can anyone hear me?
No one answered. My baby cried.
No one answered.
I began to understand
that no one may ever answer
and my baby would keep feeding
until my life was all gone.

For Yagiz, I had to stay alive.
I made pictures in my mind
of how his life should be,
of what I had planned for him,
of what I had planned for him and his brother,
and I held Yagiz safe against me
and fed him but was not able to feed myself.

Sometimes I thought I heard
footsteps, sometimes voices, sometimes drills,
but I did not know anymore if I dreamed
and I no longer screamed or called out.
Then I heard dogs barking.
Dogs barking.
I would not imagine that
but who knows what you dream
when you are buried under dust and concrete
and the world has shaken apart.

Voices. Are you okay? Voices speaking to me.
Knock once for yes. Knock once. Knock twice. Knock three times.
Can you hear me? I can hear you? Please, get me out of here.
I could hear their voices as they dug for me,
coming closer and closer, and I held
Yagiz closer and closer
and he was crying and arms reached through
and I passed Yagiz into their arms,
I let go of my baby
and listened to him crying
as they carried him away from me.

They pulled me out,
placed me on a stretcher.
And I was in the ambulance with Yagiz,
they took us together to the hospital
and I knew the faces there, they told me
my husband and my other son
had survived, they were injured to their legs,
and at another hospital but we will see them again.

Now, we are living in a tent
with eleven of my family,
with my husband and my children,
and grandparents and aunts and uncles and cousins,
because no-one has a home anymore
but we have a family
and we can move our limbs
and we can drink and we can eat
and it is cold but we keep each other warm.
We need so little to survive.

96 HOURS[10]

We have rescued 18 people from Kahramanmaras
since we arrived from Israel, but
we do not expect
to rescue more.

We did not expect to rescue many,
so many hours after the quake.
Today, we pulled a 10 year old boy out, alive.
Alive is a beautiful word to use
in this place.

We carried him out,
placed him on the stretcher
and sent him in the ambulance,
somewhere,

alone,
no family
but he will find friends
or make new friends
and there will be
a life for him.

It is what we do,
rescue people.

108 HOURS[11]

We found her with an infra-red camera
we can push into a void to get a better look.
My name is Kevin.
It is the first time I have travelled to Turkey,
knowing it is a very different country
to my home in Canada but
never imagining this.
I have trained for this,
but it is mountain rescue I do,
it is floods and fire, but beyond
the boundaries of my country, lie
this other that is still our world,
realising we are part of it all. I have trained for this.

That is how we found her, pushing through
with the camera on an articulated arm
like an alien creature in a sci-fi flick,
sneaking into her bedroom
for a quick look. Not expecting to find her
in this collapsed building, with a door on top of her,
not able to move for all these days.

Passing
food and water to her on a machinery arm
but not able to get her out
for six more hours.
Longer than the 106 already passed.
She said she was okay. Loved ones gathered,
waiting, praying, waiting, praying.
No way to lift the building off her.
So, climb in beneath the slabs of rubble
and hope it does not collapse above.

Six hours and enough space is made
to free her, so she can crawl out
from beneath the door, aided
by her rescuer's hands,
pulling her out.

Wrapped in a blanket,
bound on a stretcher,
oxygen mask attached,
shifting her through the crowd
like a rock star or a president,
a brown-haired woman
carried away in the ambulance.

And all the rescue team, the Canadian
and the Turkish and the neighbours,
band together for their selfies,
to mark this moment in time
when a woman's life was saved
and we became brothers.

When they are asked how they feel,
they say they are happy, they feel happy,
to help their Canadian friends
bring a woman out
after 108 hours.

Hugs and photos and congratulations.
And move onto the next building, can we do it again?
How many hours can a person survive
without water, food, air, movement?
I think she may have been the last.

120 HOURS[12]

We were still in shock, Cengiz and I,
holding tight to Nil and wondering
how to rebuild the stories of our lives.
We were waiting to find the body of Birce,
she was only 8 months old and had no mother's milk
to sustain her tight-fisted grip upon life
and where her cot had stood
was crushed beneath concrete.

There is a new story to tell
because minutes after the earth shook
a neighbour followed the mewling of a cat,
found Birce alive in the rubble,
she had been thrown down from the fifth floor,
she fell from the window.
Her leg was broken, her skull was broken,
there was bleeding on her brain
and no-one knew her face.
Five days in intensive care,
cared for by strangers who did not know her face
so they shared her picture on Facebook
asking if anyone knew her name.

My sister walked among the ruins
as they pulled more and more rubble away,
hoping still for a sign, for anything,
she spoke with a neighbour,
said we still looked for our baby.
I saw her being pulled out that first day,
is what the neighbour said. There was a rescue
of a baby half an hour after the quake.

We scrolled through social media,
we saw Birce's face, it was her,
we were sure it was her.
She had been taken
to Adana City Teaching and Research Hospital,
it was the largest trauma hospital in the quake zone,
and we found our way there, found our way
back to our baby.

We are a family again,
There is a picture of our family.
I am Nilay the mother,
Cengiz is the father,
Nil is the big sister,
Alin in the middle,
Birce is our baby.

There will be no more pictures
with Alin in the middle
but we praise God for giving Birce back to us
and pray that she will come home with us soon,
that she will be well enough
to come home.
We will build new stories of our lives
upward again, and Alin
will be ever in our hearts.

178 HOURS[13]

When I began working
for the Turkish Coal Operations Authority
it was not for this that I was trained,
not for digging bodies out
in an earthquake zone.

But this, this I willingly do,
pull out alive a little girl,
she might have been four years old,
maybe five, maybe six,
but she was little.

Miray, it is the most beautiful name
and she is the most beautiful girl in the world,
the most beautiful sight to see her
pulled out from that rubble
after being buried
for almost eight days.

I hope we did not frighten her
with our laughter and our cheers and our clapping
as we pulled her out from the debris, little arms
and legs hanging loosely. I could not see her face
for the hair hanging down, she was like a rag doll
but they said she was alive, and she spoke,
there was a small little voice that spoke.

I hope she is alive still.
I have not heard any more.

187 HOURS[14]

My voice is so hoarse from calling for help,
it is truly a wonder that any could hear me.
My name is Berber, I am 62 years old,
I am a diabetic.

I was trapped but I could move,
not like others I hear about
who were pinned down.
A fridge and a cabinet
kept my flat propped up
and I had an armchair to sit in
and a rug to keep me warm.
Such things seem luxuries
when I look about now
at the damage that has been done.

When the earthquake hit,
I stood up, my grandchild was still asleep,
my son turned on a light, grabbed a torch,
told me it was an earthquake. I knew already.

Then was another tremor,
the ceiling collapsed but it did not touch me.
I crouched down. My son was yelling for them all
to get out, to get away, he was yelling to me
but I did not know what he said.

I crouched, I sat down.
The wall fell over on to fridge and the cabinet.
I took the rug and pulled it over me
and I climbed into the armchair
and sat there. Waiting.
Waiting until the earth stopped shaking.

I could not hear my son anymore.
I shouted, shouted and shouted.
I shouted so much that my throat hurt.
No one heard. No one answered.

I had my medicine with me
and there was one bottle of water.
Apologies, I peed in it and let it rest.
I drank it when it got cold.
I am not ashamed.
I did what I needed to do so that I could survive.
It was the only thing to drink.
How could I not?
I did not think anyone would come to save me.
I did not know if anyone lived who could.

My son lived. My son brought three diggers.
I climbed onto the cupboard and was hitting the ceiling,
and I could see the hole in it where they were digging.
I heard a voice then and I shouted out,
and someone put their hand through the hole
and grabbed my hand. They pulled on my hand
but the hole was too small and I was scared
they would pull my arm off. But they kept pulling
and the hole was not so small after all, but still
very small and I was very scared.

I only wanted food and water then,
I wanted water to cleanse the taste of urine
from mouth, and cleanse my body
and wash away the dust
from inside and out.

I did good deeds with Allah,
I stayed in Mecca for seven years,
I did hajj and I did umra,
I did prayers for everyone,
not only for my family, I did prayers
for everyone. I think God saved me
because I did prayers for everyone.
He has saved me,
my son has saved me,
the rescuers have saved me,
the doctors have saved me, and
I have saved myself.

198 HOURS[15]

I am Muhammet, I have lived
for 17 years. I was trapped with my brother, Enes,
who is 21 years old, we were beside each other
in the rubble. Mostly, I cried for two days.
We wondered if our mother had survived.
We talked about brotherhood.
We had powdered protein to eat.
It would have been harder to be alone.
My mother did not expect
that we would both return,
but we are brothers,
together always.

201 HOURS[16]

Am I lucky?
Lucky to be trapped
in the rubble of our six storey building
for 201 hours, in those last hours
listening and more afraid than before
that it would all crash down on me
even more, that I was so close to rescue
but the closer I could hear their voices and the noise
of their tools and machines, the more afraid I became,
and I do not know the moment when they came
because the world had gone dark in my head
and nothing was happening.
Perhaps I was dead.

Then I was alive.
Then I was free.
Then there was blue sky.
Then there were smiling faces.
Then there was fluid running into my veins.
Then I was lucky.

The freedom has not lasted long.
Now I am held within these stark walls
with tubes and machines and masked strangers
working on my body like it is a car
that needs restoration.

They are monitoring my kidneys.
They are assessing what damage has been done
to my muscles and my organs and my bones and my brain.
They say I will likely have renal failure.

I say I have survived an earthquake
I say I have survived being buried alive
with the weight of the world above me
I say I have been found for a reason
I say I will teach again
I say I am lucky.

228 HOURS[17]
equals nine and a half days
beneath the rubble,
this woman and her two children.

When we pulled her out,
she asked what day it was,
and she asked for water
but nine and a half days
is a long time without water
is a long time without food
and I, Mehmet, am a rescuer
but I did not know
if she would dissolve
if I gave her anything.

We passed her over to the medics
to care for, to give her water
or what she most needed.

For nearly ten days
we have been digging,
and I am very tired
but while there are still people,
still women and children,
waiting alive beneath these rocks
and cement and debris and twisted metal,
I cannot take any rest.

The medics take them as we bring them out
and soon, I think it must be me
that will need their care.

248 HOURS[18]

I am Aleyna,
from Kahramanmaras,
I am 17 years old.
They asked me how I survived,
I just tried to pass the time on my own.
I still feel like I am trying to pass the time
on my own, though now there are others
all around me. I do not know them.
I do not know myself anymore.
They call me the miracle girl.
Am I a miracle? I am not the only one.
After me, they rescued Neslihan,
who is 30 years old, old enough
to be a wife and a mother.
Her family will help her to know who she is.
And then Osman, who is twelve,
and told the rescuers
there are more people buried alive.
Do you know what it is to be buried alive?
I do. I am Aleyna. I have been buried.
And now I am a miracle.
I hope I am not the only one.

258 HOURS[19]

I have been waiting,
waiting outside her building,
I believed she would come out,
that my daughter would return to me,
this feeling, I knew she would come back.

They had all given up, told me there was no hope
but I waited still, I knew. The forklift operator, he was
still proceeding carefully, respect for the corpses
not to be devoured by his machine. He lifted
the bed, he saw her hand move, he saw
her hand move.

258 hours, my daughter Neslihan, was returned to me.
I believed she would come out. I had a feeling.
I do not have that same feeling to tell me
that we may yet find her children, her
husband. I have no more feeling left.

260 HOURS[20]

Did you hear the applause
as they lifted me from out of the ruins
of our home in Hatay? Our home, where
we had shared so many meals, arguments, discussions,
always arguing with my family, in our apartment
that had four solid walls around it
and kept us safe
in Hatay, southernmost part
of Türkiye, so southernmost
that it might be considered northernmost
to a neighbouring country.
I am 12 years old, I know little enough,
of the politics of history and belonging to anyone
but to my family. To them I belong,
my name is Osman and
I am waiting for them to find me.
They will have heard the applause.

261 HOURS[21]

One moment, I become a father.
The next moment, I am swallowed by a hungry earth.
Bilge has just given birth to our daughter, Almila, too early
to give birth and so they had to operate, and I worried then
that our world was falling apart. But it did not
until I left them, left to buy biscuits.

I swear I will never leave them again. I have been
buried in hospital ruins, not knowing
if Almila and Bilge wait still for me
to return with biscuits, or if the world
had collapsed beneath them as well.

When they reach me, when they hear me,
when they reach me, I ask for a mobile phone.
I ring my brother. I ring my brother and ask him
to tell me the truth. Have they all survived? I say to him.
Have they all survived? Is Bilge alive, is Almila waiting
to meet her father, she was whisked away so quickly
to that incubator because she was too early,
and she had not yet grasped my finger
to tell her that her father welcomed her
and would protect her. I went to get biscuits
and was swallowed by the world collapsing
around me, over me, on me. I did not think
I would see them again. Tell me the truth, I said to my brother,
Abdulkadir, are they all alive? Have they survived?

Yes, Mustafa, he told me. They have survived.
Bilge lives, Almila waits, others we have yet to know.
Let me hear their voices, brother.
The hospital was wrecked, he tells me,
but the floor Bilge was on, with your new daughter,
it did not collapse, she was able to crawl out,
they were able to crawl out with Almila,
and she will meet her father
never know that he left her side for biscuits.

Brother, let me hear their voices.
I did not believe I would come to light again,
I did not believe I would come out,
and that if I came out,
it would be to find my wife and children dead.
I have been born again.

I have only a little pain.
I do not know how much pain is felt
by Mehmet, alongside me he was a prisoner,
he became my friend. Yet I would not know him
in the street because I have only known him
in the dark. We will find each other again,
become brothers in darkness, born again
into light, and I do not know how much pain he is in.

We did not believe we would come again
into the light and, not knowing, did not say
how we could find each other again. But we will.
If we found each other in the darkness,
we will find each other in the light.

Bilge says that our baby cried
and God heard her voice
and answered their prayers.
Thank God for giving me that strength, she says.
How I got up, how I got down, I don't know.
Now we begin our second life again. Never again will I let it go.
Bilge says it was destiny, with God everything has an order.
I look about me, I see my wife hide her pain,
our daughter crying still as though she does not know
God has answered her prayers,
she is twelve days old and the world
has not been a place of welcome.

I kiss the hand of the man who has rescued me,
the man who has loaned me his phone to ring my brother,
to ring Abdulkadir, who has been waiting by the hospital ruins
until every brick has been brought up to show there was no hope.
They told him there were no signs of life, and then there were.
My father, my brother, my wife, welcome me back to life.
My daughter, well, she cries. It is a wonderful sound.

278 HOURS

Eleven days I have lain beneath the rubble
More than 43 000 dead, I am told.
I am not among them.
I was among the missing, the unaccounted-for,
the beyond-hope, too many hours, too many days,
we cannot expect more miracles.
We can always expect miracles.
I did not ever think that
I would be called a miracle.
I am just a man, a 45 year old man,
who has lain in the rubble
of a destroyed world, waiting,
waiting for death because I believed
I was beyond hope.
Who knows where hope ends?
278 hours
and they pulled me free,
loaded me onto a stretcher,
filled my veins with saline
and I felt them swelling in gratitude
like dry river-beds at the onrush of rain.
I am alive. My name is Hakan.
I am a miracle.

288 HOURS[22]

We are still looking
though it is twelve days now
since the earth broke open.
We have come from Kyrgyzstan to search
to find our brothers and sisters
among the rubble, we think
only to find corpses
but we are digging, we hear shouts,
we pull out a Syrian family of five
but after twelve days
they are too far gone from this world,
the mother and the father survive
but the child still dies of dehydration.

A child that lives for twelve days
only to die in the hospital,
it were better to have died
on the first day
but perhaps then
the mother and the father
would not have had the will to live.
Her older sister and her twin,
they died, too.

When we heard the shouts
we were so happy,
ten ambulances waited nearby,
we blocked all the traffic,
we asked everyone for silence
and worked in complete silence
so we could find the family
with our detector, we were so happy
to find them.

And now, we are buried again
beneath the grief
as though we had crawled in to them
and never came out again. They live,
the mother and father live,
and at least there will be graves
for the little ones, graves to cover
with tears and prayers
and one day, when death comes
in old age, their parents may be reunited
with them again. And people
will place a marker on their grave,
cover them with prayers,
so they will not be forgotten
until they are. We always forget,
but God remembers
and the earth
will be forever changed.

ENDNOTES

1. Sariyuce, Isil, Yusuf Gezer, Ipek Yezdani, Mia Alberti, Christian Edwards, and Hafsa Khalil. "Turkey Halts Most Rescue Efforts for Earthquake Survivors." (20/02/2023). Egypt Independent. egyptindependent.com/turkey-halts-most-rescue-efforts-for-earthquake-survivors/.

2. Singh, Abhimav. "Two Nurses Protect a Room Full of Newborns During Turkey Earthquake." (13/02/2023). WION. www.wionews.com/trending/watch-two-nurses-protect-a-room-full-of-newborns-during-turkey-earthquake-561337.

3. "'I Think This Is the Last Video I Will Ever Shoot for You': Turkish Teen Filmed 'Last Moments' from Apartment." (19/02/2023). 9News. Sydney: AP. www.9news.com.au/world/turkish-teen-filmed-last-moments-from-quakehit-apartment/480fb9e3-a1e7-48f2-b8d2-a31256dc83d4.

4. Ibid.

5. Ibid.

6. "A Newborn Delivered in the Rubble of Turkey's Earthquake Is Adopted by Her Relatives." (February 21, 2023). www.npr.org/2023/02/21/1158520034/turkey-syria-earthquake-afraa-rubble-baby.

7. Dillinger, Katherine. "Amid Devastating Loss, Turkish Family Reunited with 'Miracle Baby' Found in Quake Rubble." CNN. (15/02/2023). edition.cnn.com/2023/02/15/health/turkey-earthquake-birce/index.html.

8. Campoamor, Danielle "Trapped for 129 Hours, a Mother and Son Survive the Devastating Earthquake in Syria." Today. (26/02/2023). www.today.com/parents/parents/trapped-129-hours-mother-son-survive-earthquake-syria-rcna70483.

9. Griffin, Allie. "Mom Recounts 4 Days of Hell Buried beneath Turkey Earthquake Rubble While Clutching Newborn." New York Post. (13/02/2023). nypost.com/2023/02/13/mom-newborn-buried-under-turkey-earthquake-rubble-for-nearly-4-days/.

10. Fabian, Emanuel "Idf Teams Rescue 10-Year-Old Boy Trapped under Rubble for 100 Hours in Turkey." (10/02/2023). www.timesofisrael.com/idf-teams-rescue-10-year-old-boy-trapped-under-rubble-for-100-hours-in-turkey/.

11. "Canadian Volunteers Help Rescue Turkish Woman Trapped for 4 Days." The National. (11/02/2023). www.youtube.com/watch?v=-J5mhVFmgIw.

12. Dillinger, Katherine. "Amid Devastating Loss, Turkish Family Reunited with 'Miracle Baby' Found in Quake Rubble." (15/02/2023). edition.cnn.com/2023/02/15/health/turkey-earthquake-birce/index.html.

13. Keane, Isabel. "More Quake Miracles." New York Post. (14/02/2023). www.pressreader.com/usa/new-york-post/20230214/281904482347461.

14 Kucukgocmen, Ali. "Defying Odds: A Story of Survival under Turkey's Earthquake Rubble." (16/02/2023). www.reuters.com/world/middle-east/defying-odds-story-survival-under-turkeys-earthquake-rubble-2023-02-15/.

15 Keane, Isabel. "Brothers Trapped under Rubble for Nearly 200 Hours Rescued after Turkey Earthquake." New York Post. (14/02/2023). nypost.com/2023/02/14/brothers-trapped-for-nearly-200-hours-rescued-in-turkey-earthquake/.

16 Lynch, Cordelia, Kirsty Hickey, and Guldenay Sonumu. "Turkey Earthquake: Teacher Rescued after 200 Hours under Rubble – as Baby Survives Falling Five Floors." (14/02/2023). news.sky.com/story/turkey-earthquake-teacher-rescued-after-200-hours-under-rubble-as-baby-survives-falling-five-floors-12811088.

17 Panella, Chris. "A Woman Who Survived for 9 Days under the Rubble of Turkey's Deadly Earthquake Didn't Know What Day It Was When She Was Rescued and Immediately Asked for Water." Insider. (16/02/2023). www.insider.com/turkey-earthquake-woman-survived-9-days-under-rubble-2023-2.

18 Alam, Hande Atay, Isil Sariyuce, and Sana Noor Haq. "Three Survivors Pulled Alive from Earthquake Rubble in Turkey, More Than 248 Hours after Quake." (16/02/2023). edition.cnn.com/2023/02/16/europe/turkey-syria-earthquake-rescue-efforts-intl/index.html.

19 Ibid.

20 "12-Year-Old Boy Rescued after '260 Hours' under Rubble, Authorities Say." HeraldSun. (17/02/2023). www.heraldsun.com.au/news/national/12yearold-boy-rescued-after-260-hours-under-rubble-authorities-say/video/b4f654d18ade3ade0092e2ed08ce7c4a.

21 Young, Andrew. "'I Never Thought I Would Come out' Survivor of Turkey's Earthquake Who Was Reunited with His Wife and Newborn Baby after Being Trapped in Hospital Ruins for 261 Hours Tells of His Battle to Stay Alive." Daily Mail Australia. (21/02/2023). www.dailymail.co.uk/news/article-11773141/Turkey-earthquake-survivor-trapped-ruins-261-hours-tells-battle-stay-alive.html.

22 "Turkey Earthquake Rescue Operations to End, Government Says." (19/02/2023). www.aljazeera.com/news/2023/2/19/earthquake-rescue-operations-ended-in-most-turkey-provinces-afad.

www.ingramcontent.com/pod-product-compliance
Lightning Source LLC
Chambersburg PA
CBHW040244010526
44107CB00065B/2867